COLLEGE SPORTS TODAY

COLLEGE SPORTS TODAY

BIG RED!

THE NEBRASKA CORNHUSKERS STORY

JOHN NICHOLS

CREATIVE EDUCATION

Published by Creative Education
123 South Broad Street, Mankato, Minnesota 56001
Creative Education is an imprint of The Creative Company

Designed by Stephanie Blumenthal
Production design by The Design Lab
Editorial assistance by John Nichols

Photos by: Allsport USA, AP/Wide World Photos,
SportsChrome, and UPI/Corbis-Bettmann

Library of Congress Cataloging-in-Publication Data

Nichols, John, 1966–
Big Red! the Nebraska Cornhuskers story / by John Nichols.
p. cm. — (College football today)
Summary: Highlights some of the important personalities and key moments in
football played at the University of Nebraska.
ISBN: 0-88682-980-1

1. Nebraska Cornhuskers (Football team)—Juvenile literature. 2. University of Nebraska—Lincoln—
Football—History—Juvenile literature. [1. Nebraska Cornhuskers (Football team)—History.
2. Football—History.] I. Title. II. Series: College football today (Mankato, Minn.)

GV958.U53N53   1999
796.332'63'09782293—dc21   98-46472

First Edition

2 4 6 8 9 7 5 3 1

n certain autumn afternoons, the powerful prairie winds that howl over America's Midwest carry the unmistakable sounds of college football: the popping of pads, the ferocious growls of battling players, and the mighty roar of cheering fans. In Lincoln, Nebraska, home of the five-time national champion University of Nebraska Cornhuskers, the pads pop louder, the players battle harder, and the cheers reach deafening levels. For more than 100 years, the winds that carry their exploits have sounded an alarm to those who would dare challenge them: "Today you are playing the University of Nebraska, and nobody beats Big Red."

SPEEDY QUARTERBACK

BOBBY NEWCOMBE IS

ALWAYS DANGEROUS.

SPLIT END KENNY

CHEATHAM (ABOVE);

NEBRASKA FOOTBALL—

A CHAMPIONSHIP

ATTITUDE (BELOW)

LAWRENCE PHILLIPS HEADED NEBRASKA'S 1995 CHAMPIONSHIP RUN.

After the short season, Frothingham left the school to return home to Boston. Fortunately for Nebraska, the good professor left his football in Lincoln.

After Frothingham's departure, the popularity of football in Nebraska grew like the tall shocks of corn that shoot up from the state's black soil. In those early years, the football team had several nicknames, including the Tree-planters, Rattlesnake Boys, Antelopes, Old Gold Knights, and Bugeaters. In 1899, Charles "Cy" Sherman, sports editor for the *Nebraska State Journal*, dubbed the team the "Cornhuskers," and the name stuck. At the turn of the century, Nebraska changed its school colors to scarlet and cream, and its football program began its rapid rise to national prominence.

THE 'HUSKERS SADDLE THE HORSEMEN

Between 1915 and 1925, America grew and matured a great deal as a nation. World War I had been fought and won, the economy was booming, and the United States was beginning to realize its awesome strength and influence.

The same could be said for the University of Nebraska football team during that period. The Cornhuskers quickly grew from their humble roots to become one of the true gridiron power-houses in the Midwest. Unfortunately, America's football focus at the time lay mainly on teams from the more-populated East and South. Nebraska yearned to earn the respect of the

entire nation, and they knew that to do so, they would have to beat the best: Notre Dame.

Nebraska battled the powerful Fighting Irish of Notre Dame 11 times between 1915 and 1925. With each meeting, the rivalry grew more intense. The highlight of the series came in 1923, when Notre Dame was led by legendary coach Knute Rockne and featured an offensive backfield so awesome that the players became known as "The Four Horsemen."

Notre Dame came to Lincoln on November 10, 1923, bent on avenging a 14–6 loss suffered the year before. The Irish were 6–0 and had held their opponents to one touchdown or less in every game. Nebraska, on the other hand, came into the game with a mere 1–1–2 record. All signs pointed to a Notre Dame runaway victory, but Nebraska coach Fred Dawson had his team thinking upset in its first game in the school's new Memorial Stadium.

The defenses dominated early on, but in the second quarter, Nebraska's Dave "Big Moose" Noble took a handoff and tore through the left side of the Notre Dame line for a 24-yard touchdown. Later, in the fourth quarter, Noble caught a short pass on Notre Dame's 5-yard line. Though hit immediately, Noble stayed upright. He lunged free from the weary Notre Dame defenders and scored the game-clinching touchdown, upsetting the heavily favored Irish 14–7.

QUARTERBACK TURNER

GILL (ABOVE); COACH

BOB DEVANEY (LEFT)

I-BACK AHMAN GREEN RAN ROUGHSHOD OVER OPPONENTS IN THE '90S.

The Nebraska-Notre Dame rivalry brought fame to both schools. After 11 contests in 11 bruising years, the teams stood dead even at 5–5–1. But in 1925, the series ended. The rivalry had grown too bitter to continue. No one, however, could deny the great moments that the series provided. "What a magnificent test of wills these games have been," exclaimed Notre Dame's Rockne. "Both teams have certainly got their licks in."

During the remainder of the 1920s and '30s, the Corn-huskers' winning record brought pride to Nebraskans suffering through the Great Depression and the Dust Bowl. All-Americans such as fullback Sam Francis, guard Warren Alfson, and tackle Forrest Behm kept Big Red rolling until 1940, when Nebraska accepted a bid to play in the school's first bowl game. Nebraska met Stanford in the Rose Bowl on January 1, 1941.

The Cornhuskers lost to Stanford 21–13, but Nebraska was so excited to be in the game that it felt like a win. Years later, Hall of Fame coach and former Nebraska athletic director Bob Devaney joked, "I coached here for a long time before I found out that we had lost the 1941 Rose Bowl."

After the Rose Bowl, however, the Cornhuskers' fortunes took a turn for the worse. Nine straight losing seasons followed as Nebraskans, like all Americans, turned their attention toward World War II.

RUNNING BACK LAWRENCE

PHILLIPS (ABOVE); COACH

TOM OSBORNE (BELOW)

NAME: Sam Francis

POSITION: Fullback

SEASONS PLAYED: 1934–1936

AWARDS/HONORS: All-Big Six Conference selection (1935, 1936), All-American (1936), National Football Foundation Hall of Fame inductee

Francis was one of the founding fathers of Nebraska's tradition of exceptional running backs. His heroics, along with those of his Cornhuskers teammates, were a steady source of encouragement for Nebraskans struggling through the Great Depression in the 1930s. In 1935 and 1936, the fullback led Nebraska to a combined 9–0–1 conference record and two Big Six Conference titles. In his final season, he helped the Cornhuskers outscore their opponents by a 185–49 margin and became the ninth Nebraska player to earn All-American honors. His football achievements were recognized at the highest level 41 years later when he was inducted into the National Football Foundation Hall of Fame.

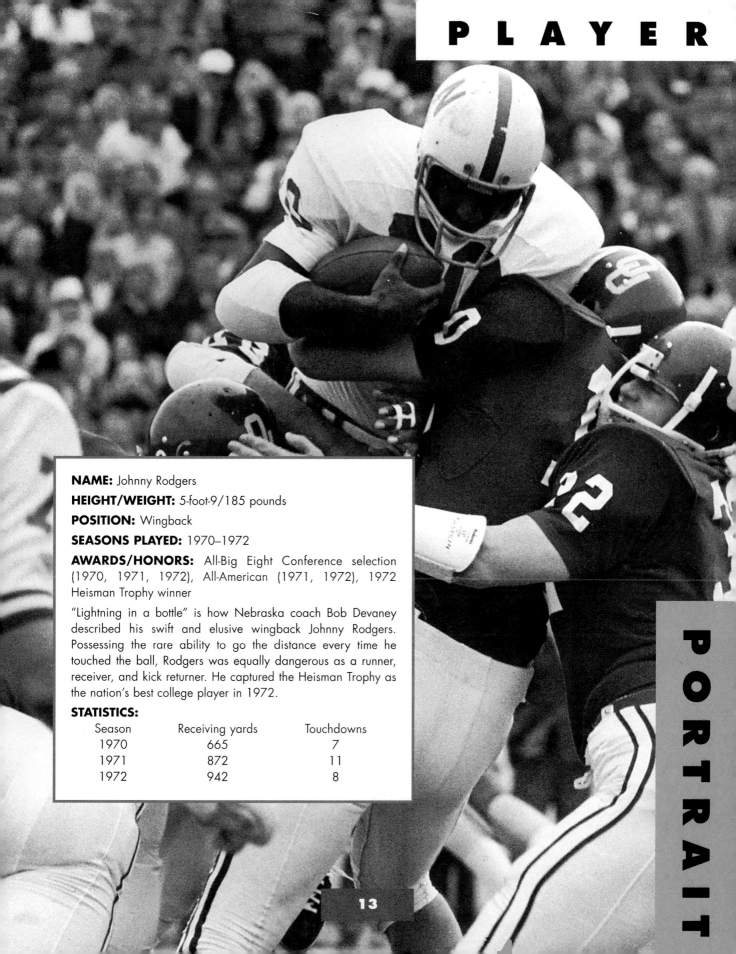

NAME: Johnny Rodgers

HEIGHT/WEIGHT: 5-foot-9/185 pounds

POSITION: Wingback

SEASONS PLAYED: 1970–1972

AWARDS/HONORS: All-Big Eight Conference selection (1970, 1971, 1972), All-American (1971, 1972), 1972 Heisman Trophy winner

"Lightning in a bottle" is how Nebraska coach Bob Devaney described his swift and elusive wingback Johnny Rodgers. Possessing the rare ability to go the distance every time he touched the ball, Rodgers was equally dangerous as a runner, receiver, and kick returner. He captured the Heisman Trophy as the nation's best college player in 1972.

STATISTICS:

Season	Receiving yards	Touchdowns
1970	665	7
1971	872	11
1972	942	8

RECENT QUARTERBACKS

BROOK BERRINGER

(ABOVE) AND TOMMIE

FRAZIER (BELOW)

REAWAKENING THE THUNDER

Despite a brief resurgence in the early 1950s, highlighted by standout tailback Bobby Reynolds' 1,342 rushing yards in 1950, winning football would not return to Lincoln until 1962. That year, a fiery coach from the University of Wyoming came in to turn the program around. His name was Bob Devaney.

The hard-driving Devaney wasted little time in sending his team a message, putting increased emphasis on improving the team's strength and conditioning. The hard work paid off as the previously underachieving Cornhuskers blossomed into a confident winner in 1962.

Sparked by the play of quarterback Dennis Claridge, running back Bill "Thunder" Thornton, and All-American lineman Bob Brown, Nebraska posted a 9–2 record that included the school's first bowl game victory: a 36–34 defeat of the University of Miami in the now-defunct Gotham Bowl.

In his first five seasons (1962–66), Devaney's 'Huskers rolled to a 47–8 record and five straight bowl appearances. But

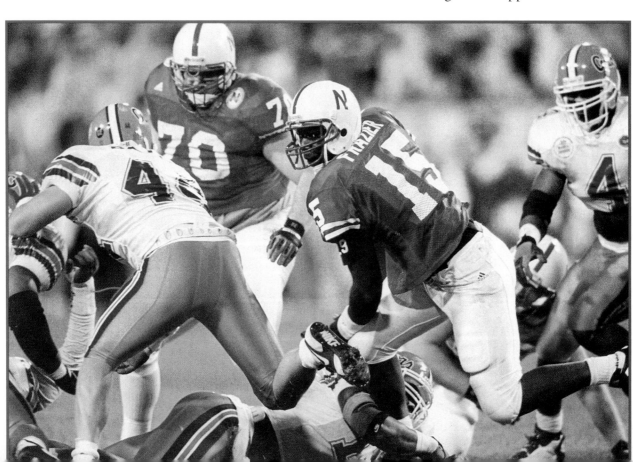

AHMAN GREEN, A DANGEROUS 'HUSKERS BACK

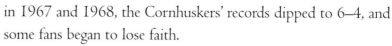

in 1967 and 1968, the Cornhuskers' records dipped to 6–4, and some fans began to lose faith.

Devaney's frustration with the team's sluggish performance led him to a fateful decision. At the suggestion of offensive coordinator Tom Osborne, Devaney junked the team's offensive scheme and installed the I-formation. This formation positions the halfback and fullback directly behind the quarterback before the snap, making it harder for defenses to predict where the play is going. The new offense focused on a power running game. In order to make it work, the 'Huskers needed large, athletic linemen and game-breaking running backs. Luckily for Devaney and Cornhuskers fans, they had both.

TRIPLE-THREAT RODGERS AND DOUBLE CHAMPIONSHIPS

After watching game film of Omaha Tech high school football star Johnny Rodgers, Bob Devaney turned to his assistants and said, "If we don't keep this kid here in Nebraska, they [the fans] will never forgive us."

Fortunately, Rodgers chose Nebraska and provided Devaney with the multi-purpose offensive weapon he needed. The 5-foot-10 and 180-pound Rodgers combined great speed with the ability to

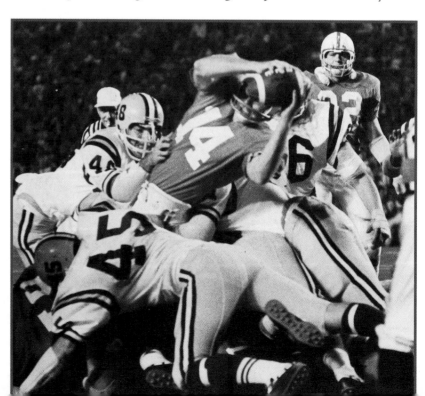

change direction almost instantly. After learning the system in 1969 (freshmen were not eligible to play varsity sports at that time), Rodgers and the 'Huskers took the football world by storm in 1970. Playing wingback—a combination receiver/running back—Rodgers dazzled opponents with his rushing, receiving, kick returns, and even passing. "Johnny does it all for Nebraska," said rival running back Greg Pruitt of the Oklahoma Sooners. "But you can't stop him because you don't know where he'll be coming from next."

Rodgers scored 11 touchdowns in 12 games his sophomore season to power the 'Huskers to an 11–0–1 record. They completed an undefeated season with a 17–12 victory over Louisiana State in the Orange Bowl on New Year's Day. When the postseason polls came out, Nebraska was declared national champion by the Associated Press. "It's quite an honor," said a proud Devaney. "The people of Nebraska truly deserve this."

Nebraska got even better in 1971. Rodgers electrified fans, scoring 17 touchdowns through a combination of rushing, receiving, and returning kicks. Star quarterback Jerry Tagge gave the 'Huskers polished passing and strong leadership, and offensive

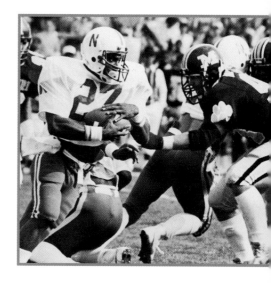

RECEIVER IRVING FRYAR,

ONE OF THE '83

"TRIPLETS" (ABOVE);

MIKE ROZIER (BELOW)

lineman Larry Jacobsen anchored a massive, mobile line. The Cornhuskers cruised through their schedule, demolishing opponents by 20 to 30 points a game.

Nebraska was so dominant that even longtime nemesis, and next-door neighbor, Oklahoma could not stand in Big Red's way. Sparked by Rodgers's electrifying first-quarter punt return for a touchdown, Nebraska came away with a hard-fought, 35–31 win over the second-ranked Sooners on November 25. The victory earned the 'Huskers a trip to the 1972 Orange Bowl against the Alabama Crimson Tide. There, the Cornhuskers obliterated Bear Bryant's then-unbeaten Alabama team 38–6 to clinch their second straight national championship and a perfect 13–0 season. In light of that impressive win, many experts consider the 1971 Cornhuskers the greatest college football team ever assembled.

With Rodgers returning, Nebraska was a heavy favorite to repeat again as national champs the following season. Unfortunately for 'Huskers fans, Nebraska's bid for a third consecutive championship fell short in 1972. A season-opening loss to UCLA ended Nebraska's 32-game unbeaten streak. Rodgers, however, contributed yet another incredible season, scoring 17 touchdowns on 308 yards rushing, 942 yards receiving, and 802 yards in kick returns. With his incredible numbers, Rodgers earned the Heisman Trophy as the nation's outstanding player. "Johnny is just one fantastic young man and football player," said Devaney. "It was a pleasure to coach him."

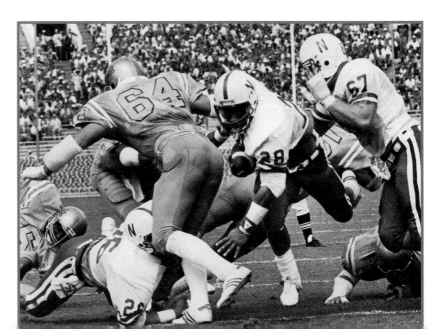

DR. TOM TAKES THE REINS

With Johnny Rodgers in professional football and Bob Devaney stepping down from coaching to become Nebraska's athletic director, many experts predicted a slide in the program's performance. New coach Tom Osborne, a native of Hastings, Nebraska, had other thoughts. The quiet, scholarly coach personified the Midwestern ideals that Nebraskans hold dear: hard work, dedication, and selflessness. Osborne, who earned a doctorate degree in education psychology from Nebraska in 1965, kept the 'Huskers' victory party running. In Osborne's first 21 seasons, Nebraska won at least nine games per season.

Osborne's teams featured overwhelming running attacks sparked by speedsters such as I. M. Hipp and Jarvis Redwine. On the defensive side, the 'Huskers had bone-crushing hitters such as All-American tackle John Dutton and end Neil Smith.

Under Osborne, Nebraska emphasized weight training to make players bigger, faster, and stronger. Nebraska also developed an extensive "walk on" program in which high school players were encouraged to try to make the team without the promise of a scholarship.

These innovations kept Nebraska among the nation's elite, but year after year there was one team that Nebraska could not beat: arch rival Oklahoma. In Osborne's first five seasons, Oklahoma spoiled the Cornhuskers' national championship hopes every time.

When Nebraska finally beat Oklahoma in 1978, the program gained momentum. By the early 1980s, Nebraska's hopes ran high for another national championship.

SPEEDY I-BACK DEANGELO

EVANS: THE NEXT GREAT

'HUSKERS BACK

PORTRAIT

NAME: Tom Osborne

BORN: February 23, 1937

POSITION: Head Coach

SEASONS COACHED: 1973–1997 (1962–1972 as assistant coach)

AWARDS/HONORS: Fifth winningest coach by percentage in NCAA Division 1–A history (.836), 13 conference championships, three national championships, 25 bowl game appearances

RECORD: 255–49–3

Nebraska native Tom Osborne provided 25 years of rock-solid stability as head coach of the Nebraska Cornhuskers. In his quarter-century at the helm, his teams never failed to win at least nine games a season. He led the 'Huskers to six conference titles and two national championships in his last seven seasons on the sidelines. Osborne's quiet nature masked an intense commitment to excellence, both on the football field and in the classroom, and Nebraska produced 46 Academic All-Americans during his tenure. In 1998, Memorial Stadium was renamed Tom Osborne Stadium in his honor.

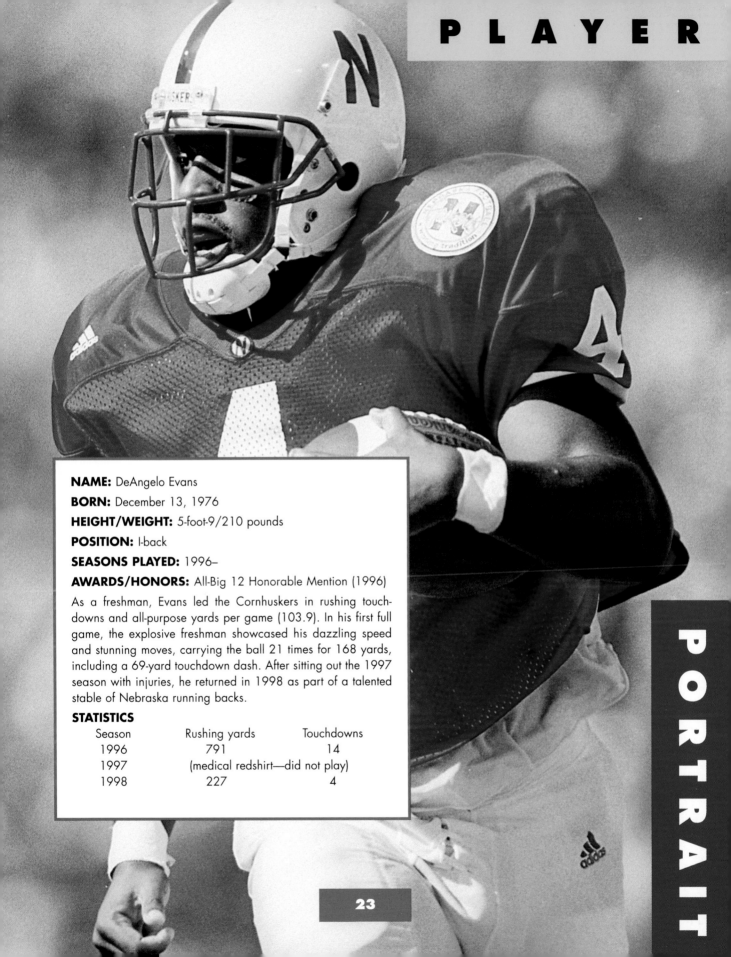

NAME: DeAngelo Evans

BORN: December 13, 1976

HEIGHT/WEIGHT: 5-foot-9/210 pounds

POSITION: I-back

SEASONS PLAYED: 1996–

AWARDS/HONORS: All-Big 12 Honorable Mention (1996)

As a freshman, Evans led the Cornhuskers in rushing touchdowns and all-purpose yards per game (103.9). In his first full game, the explosive freshman showcased his dazzling speed and stunning moves, carrying the ball 21 times for 168 yards, including a 69-yard touchdown dash. After sitting out the 1997 season with injuries, he returned in 1998 as part of a talented stable of Nebraska running backs.

STATISTICS

Season	Rushing yards	Touchdowns
1996	791	14
1997	(medical redshirt—did not play)	
1998	227	4

PORTRAIT

NEBRASKA'S TERRIFYING "TRIPLETS"

The 1983 Nebraska team featured one of the most potent offenses in college football history. All-American guard Dean Steinkuhler blew open holes for a trio of skilled offensive players: speedy receiver Irving Fryar, lightning-quick quarterback Turner Gill, and powerful I-back Mike Rozier. These three formed the "Triplets," an unstoppable, three-headed demolition crew. The Cornhuskers regularly rolled over opponents by 30, 40, or even 50 points. Rozier led the charge, rushing for 2,148 yards and scoring an amazing 29 touchdowns. The mighty Cornhuskers bashed their way to a 12–0 regular season mark and a berth in the Orange Bowl against the University of Miami.

Early in that Orange Bowl game, Miami, led by standout quarterback Bernie Kosar, built a 17-point lead. But the 'Huskers refused to fold and battled back. With 48 seconds left on the clock, Nebraska I-back Jeff Smith rumbled in for a touchdown, shaving Miami's lead to 31–30. Coach Osborne faced a tough decision. Should he kick the extra point for the tie—which might be enough to clinch the national championship—or go for two to win the game outright? Osborne chose to go for two. Moments later, Gill's pass to Smith was tipped away, and Nebraska lost the game and the national championship to Miami. Osborne, however, earned the respect of fans everywhere by going for the win rather than settling for a tie.

Although Nebraska did not reach its goal of a championship, team members did earn a host of individual awards. Rozier captured the Heisman Trophy on the strength of his phenomenal season. Steinkuhler received the Outland Trophy and Lombardi Trophy for his line play, and Osborne was named Coach of the Year. Still, Osborne's 'Huskers had not won the big game. Some fans began to wonder if the team ever would.

LINEMAN ZACH WIEGERT

(ABOVE); DAMON

BENNING (BELOW)

RECLAIMING THE CROWN

The painful 1984 Orange Bowl defeat began another period during which Nebraska would dominate most teams but struggle with others. In the 1970s, Oklahoma was the obstacle. In the 1980s and early '90s, it was Miami and Florida State. These

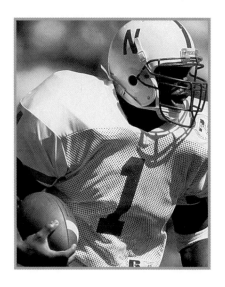

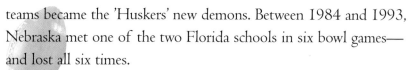

teams became the 'Huskers' new demons. Between 1984 and 1993, Nebraska met one of the two Florida schools in six bowl games—and lost all six times.

The script for defeat seemed the same each year. The pro-style passing offenses of the Florida schools shredded Nebraska's bigger but slower defenses. By building early leads, the Florida powerhouses forced the Cornhuskers out of their game. When Nebraska had to drop its running game and pass in an effort to score points quickly, the team was no match for either school. The Cornhuskers' championship hopes wilted like Nebraska corn under a hot Florida sun.

The 1994 season started well, but injuries to starting quarterback Tommie Frazier and backup Brook Berringer forced Nebraska to overcome a great deal of adversity. The 'Huskers finished the regular season 12–0 and once again faced the University of Miami—this time in the 1995 Orange Bowl.

Many experts again predicted doom for Nebraska. When Miami streaked to a 17–7 lead, it seemed another season would be ruined. Nebraska, however, refused to fade. Led by an earth-shaking offensive line and a swarming defense, the 'Huskers crushed Miami in the second half, scoring 17 unanswered points to win 24–17. "This breaks the hex," shouted jubilant Outland Trophy-winning offensive tackle Zach Wiegert. "These guys have

owned us, and now we own them." With the victory, Nebraska captured its first national championship in 23 years and its first under Coach Osborne.

REPEATING THE FEAT

With nearly all of its starters returning, including senior quarterback and leader Tommie Frazier, Nebraska was an overwhelming favorite to repeat the next season. "Tommie's the key for us because he is extremely creative and explosive, but he doesn't turn the ball over," noted Osborne. "He puts incredible pressure on defenses." Frazier, along with I-backs Lawrence Phillips and Ahman Green, took turns running roughshod over the opposition. Meanwhile, the "Blackshirt" defense—so named because Nebraska's defensive starters wear black jerseys in practice—led by Jared Tomich and Grant Wistrom, stopped teams cold.

After an 11–0 regular season, the 'Huskers had only one obstacle left between them and another national championship: the University of Florida Gators. The Gators' "Fun and Gun" pass offense had shot down defenses all season long. Frazier and Phillips had plans of their own, however. They spearheaded a bruising ground assault that hammered the Gators into submission. The final score of 62–24 represented one of the most dominating performances in Fiesta Bowl history. Nebraska was number one again.

In 1996, Nebraska's bid for a national championship "threepeat" was snuffed out by a 37–27 Big 12 conference loss to Texas. "We overlooked them, and they made us pay, " disappointed I-back Ahman Green said. "It was a hard lesson to learn."

With the sting of the Texas defeat still fresh, Coach Osborne and the 'Huskers set out to redeem themselves in 1997.

ANOTHER GREAT

NEBRASKA QUARTERBACK:

BOBBY NEWCOMBE

Led by Green and quarterback Scott Frost on offense and Jason Peter, Grant Wistrom, and Jared Tomich on defense, Nebraska steamrolled to eight straight blowout victories. Only the upstart Missouri Tigers—who had not beaten Nebraska since 1978—remained to derail the Big Red juggernaut.

The Tigers forgot about their losing history. Instead, they shocked the 'Huskers faithful by building a 38–31 lead with 1:02 left in the game. "We were in a dog fight," Frost said.

Sixty-seven yards from the tying score, Frost coolly marched the offense to the Tigers' 12 yard-line. With an entire season on the line, Frost dropped back and fired a pass into the end zone that bounced out of wingback Shelvin Wiggins's hands. The tumbling ball then deflected off of Wiggins's foot, past two Missouri defenders, and into the hands of diving Nebraska receiver Matt Davison. The Cornhuskers had needed a miracle, and they got one.

Given new life and spurred on by Osborne's surprise announcement that he would retire at the season's end, the 'Huskers beat Missouri in overtime 45–38 and powered their way to an Orange Bowl berth against number-three ranked Tennessee. Frost again led the way, scoring on two runs as Big Red rolled over the Volunteers 42–17.

Following their Orange Bowl victory, the 'Huskers earned a share of the national title by climbing to number one in the coaches' poll (Michigan finished first in the Associated Press poll). "I'm very proud of these young men," said an emotionally-spent Osborne. "They made my last season as coach a very memorable one."

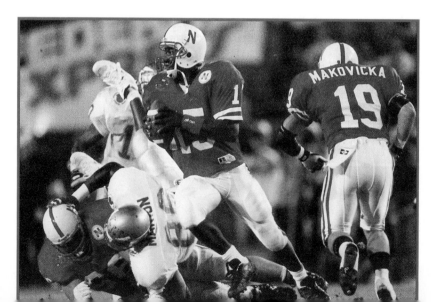

OUTLAND TROPHY WINNER ZACH WIEGERT.

Replacing a coach such as Tom Osborne is a daunting task that might scare off many people, but not Frank Solich. "I have been preparing to coach this football team for a long time, and I'm excited about the challenge," Solich said.

Solich's Nebraska football roots trace back to the mid-1960s, when he played fullback for Bob Devaney. His intense, bruising style belied the fact that he weighed less than 160 pounds. "You could see early on [that] Frank had an inner drive that was going to make him special," Osborne said.

Although Solich's 'Huskers won nine games during the 1998 season, they also suffered tough losses to Texas, Texas A&M, and Kansas State that knocked them out of contention for the national title. Nebraska's bid to win its fifth straight bowl game also came up short when the Cornhuskers fell to the Arizona Wildcats 23–20 in the Holiday Bowl. The defeat sent Nebraska to its first four-loss season in 30 years.

Despite some recent setbacks, the future of Nebraska football under Solich looks bright. Speedy I-back DeAngelo Evans and flashy quarterback Bobby Newcombe look to spark the offense, while nose tackle Steve Warren and hard-hitting rover Mike Brown will anchor the Blackshirt defense.

Whether this new generation of 'Huskers can match the brilliance of the school's past heroes remains to be seen, but it is also part of the fun of Cornhusker football. The names may change and the coaches may come and go, but in the minds of Nebraska fans, one thing remains the same: nobody beats Big Red.

COACH FRANK SOLICH

LOOKS TO DUPLICATE THE

SUCCESS OF TOM OSBORNE.